WESTWARD HO
CONCORD COACH - STAGING AND FREIGHTING

BROUGHT TO YOU BY

The books created by Equine Heritage Institute are designed to preserve the history and majesty of the horse. Our goal is to find, understand, and pass on the valuable data about equine use and its influence on humanity. The Equine Heritage Institute is a not for profit 503(c) and 100% of all proceeds from the sale of books, services, and products support Equine Heritage Institute's mission.

To make a donation to EHI, please visit www.ehi-donations.com

SPECIAL THANKS TO OUR TEAM

Mary Chris Foxworthy, Research Writer

Mary Chris Foxworthy's grandfather owned one of the last creameries in the United States that still used horse-drawn milk wagons. This sparked Mary's life-long love affair with horses and passion for keeping their history alive. After graduating from college with a degree in Food Science and Communications, Mary Chris bought her very first horse with her very first paycheck. Since then, she has served on the board of various equine associations and held a judge's card in Carriage Driving. She is known for her work in the Gloria Austin Collection, and has published and presented numerous equine educational programs. She has written for several equine publications and won an award from American Horse Publications for one of her articles. Mary Chris is an active exhibitor in Carriage Driving and Dressage. Along with her husband, she enjoys spending time with their horses (three Morgans and a PRE), a bouncing Bearded Collie and two adult children.

Taylor Murray, Editor

Taylor Murray is a copy editor and creative writer who currently resides in Ocala, FL; also known as The Horse Capital of the World. Taylor is a professional in the Hospitality industry as an Event Planner, but her passion has always been writing. In 2015, she graduated from Florida Gulf Coast University with a bachelor's degree in Hospitality Management and a Minor in Creative Writing. After a few years of making sure hotel rooms were booked and parties were planned, she decided to pursue her passion in writing. Since then, she has written for business websites, completed her first collection of poetry, and hopes to one day publish a novel based on her life.

Abby David, Graphic Designer

Abby David's family has roots in the Walking Horse tradition and she grew up hearing tales of Ole Tobe the mule's antics, holiday wagon decorations, and trick riding. She landed a job as a Graphic Designer at The Arts Center of Cannon County in 2004 and has worked in the print and digital mass communications industry continuously. Since marrying into a family in the racehorse business, David Racing Stables and Ortiz Racing Stables, she has enjoyed exploring a whole new world of horses and wearing big fancy hats. She also enjoys dancing in all it's forms and teaches in her local community.

Gloria Austin's Collection of Books

www.GloriaAustin.com

ENJOY OUR OTHER BOOKS

- How a Horse Can Make You a Better Dancer
- The Brewster Story
- Carriage Lamps
- Gloria Austin's Carriage Collection
- A Glossary of Harness Parts
- Equine Elegance
- The Fire Horse
- Horse Basics 101
- The Unsung Heros of World War One
- The Horse, History, and Human Culture
- Horse Symbolism
- Horses of the Americas
- A Drive Through Time: Carriages, Horses, and History
- Speak Your Horse's Language
- Tea: Steeped in Tradition
- The Golden Carriage and the House of Hapsburg

Brought To You By The Equine Heritage Institute

Westward Ho
By: Gloria Austin President of Equine Heritage Institute, Inc. (EHI)

First Publish Date 2019
Copyright © 2019 by Equine Heritage Institute, Inc.

All rights reserved. No part of this publication may be reproduced, distributed, or transmitted in any form or by any means, including photocopying, recording, or other electronic or mechanical methods, without the prior written permission of the publisher, except in the case of brief quotations embodied in critical reviews and certain other noncommercial uses permitted by copyright law. For permission requests, write to the publisher, addressed "Attention: Permissions Coordinator," at the address below.

Gloria Austin Carriage Collection, LLC; Equine Heritage Institute, Inc.
3024 Marion County Road Weirsdale, FL 32195 Office: (352) 753-2826 Fax: (352) 753-6186

Ordering Information:
Quantity sales: Special discounts are available on quantity purchases by corporations, associations, and others. For details, contact the publisher at the address above.
Printed in the United States of America First Edition ISBN
ISBN: 978-1-7339860-5-2 - Print, ISBN: 978-1-7339860-6-9 - E-book

TABLE OF CONTENTS

Sea to Shining Sea 8
    The Lure of the West 10
        Spreading the Faith 11
        Gold! 12
        Free land 13
    Inching Westward 14
    On your mark...get set... 15
    Go! 16

Westward Ho! 21
    The Needs 22
    Getting Supplies and People to the West 24
        Commercial Freighters 26
        Military Freighters 36

Getting Around in the West 43
    A Stagecoach for Every Purpose 46
        Mud Wagon 47
        Celerity Wagon 48
        Mountain Wagon 49
        Observation Wagon 50
        Transfer Omnibus 51
        Concord Coach 52
    Stagecoach Travel - Good to Know! 53

Abbott and Downing 56
    The Deadwood Coach 58

Anatomy of a Stagecoach 60
    The Austin Coach 64

Colorful Characters 73
    Mountain Men 74
    The Pony Express 76
    Stagecoach Guards and Drivers 78
    Wild West Shows 82
    The Reality 84

Glossary 87
Sources 89

SEA TO SHINING SEA

After the American Revolution, the American economy was in quite a shambles yet, the young country was destined to grow. Congress knew that it needed to establish an orderly and equitable procedure for the settlement and political incorporation of the Northwest Territory. The Northwest Ordinance of 1787 laid the basis for the government of the Northwest Territory and for the admission of states into the union. The Ordinance spurred westward migration by opening land in the west to be developed. People left their homes in the East in search of economic opportunity. Many of these pioneers associated westward migration, land ownership, and farming with freedom. The western frontier offered the possibility of independence and upward mobility for all! The pioneers encountered many hardships on their journey west and, once settled into the vast new land, they needed to be able to travel from town to town and to get supplies.

Slowly, the map of a continent spanning nation was forming.

John Gast, American Progress, 1872.

The phrase, 'Manifest Destiny', expressed the belief that the United States was destined to expand from the Atlantic seaboard to the Pacific Ocean. The term was used in the 1840s to mean apparent and inexorable right to expand the territories of the United States. It was a general notion rather than specific policy.

THE LURE OF THE WEST

In 1682, René-Robert Cavelier, Sieur de La Salle claimed the territory drained by the Mississippi River and its tributaries for France. He named it the Louisiana Territory.

The expedition of Lewis and Clark in 1804 impacted America's imagination and desire to start a new life in the west. Meriwether Lewis and William Clark led a party across the wilderness acquired by the Louisiana Purchase in and through the Oregon Country. During their 7,689 mile, 28-month journey they made the first U.S. crossing from the Missouri River to the Pacific coast. Their expedition bolstered the U.S. claim to the Oregon Country, purchased from England 40 years later.

Surveyors, naturalists, artists and settlers soon followed. Trail blazers and mountain men led the way for covered wagons. They were instrumental in opening up the various trails that eventually widened into wagon roads allowing Americans in the east to settle the new territories of the far west. The mountain men and the big fur companies originally opened these routes to serve the fur trade.

Eventually, organized wagon trains of settlers ventured over these roads to settle the American West.

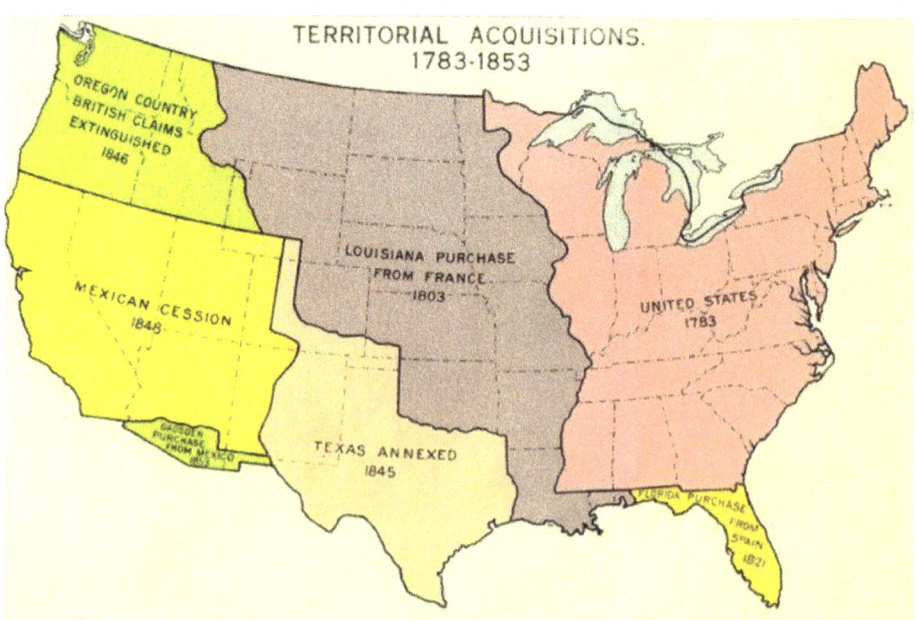

SPREADING THE FAITH

Spreading of the Christian faith also brought people to the west. When the American Revolution was raging in the east, a Franciscan monk was establishing missions throughout California. Saint Junípero Serra is known as the "Apostle of California" and "The Father of the California Missions". In 1773, he convinced the authorities in Mexico City to increase support for expansion of the missions. He also urged Spanish officials to establish an overland route to Alta California. Alta California was the name for Upper California under the Viceroyalty of New Spain. Early in the year 1769, Junipero Serra accompanied Governor Gaspar de Portolà on his expedition to Alta California. When the party reached San Diego on July 1, Father Serra stayed behind to start the Mission San Diego de Alcalá, the first of the 21 California missions founded under Serra's leadership. He was canonized as a saint by Pope Francis when the Pope came to the United States in 2015.

El Camino Real was the Spanish name for "The Royal Road." This 600 miles was also known as "The Kings Highway" or "California Mission Trail" and is now Route 101. The road connected 21 Missions, presidios, and several pueblos stretching from Mission San Diego de Alcalá in San Diego in the south to Mission San Francisco Solano in Sonoma in the north.

Las California was later a territory and department of Mexico and consisted of the modern American states of California, Nevada, Arizona, Utah, New Mexico, western Colorado, and southwestern Wyoming. The territory passed to American control after the Mexican–American War and ceased to exist with the creation of the State of California in 1850.

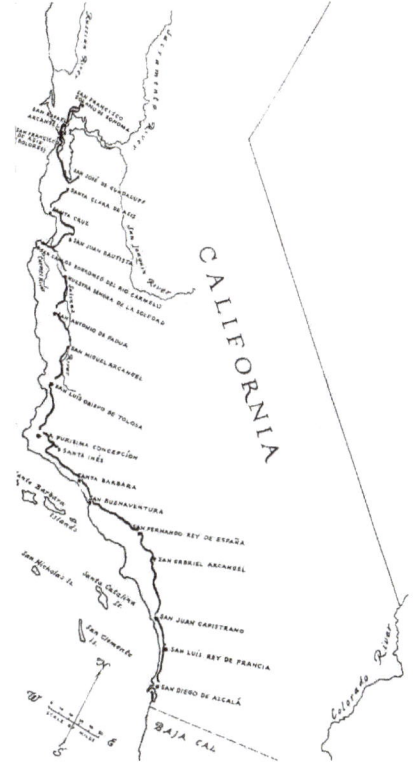

GOLD!

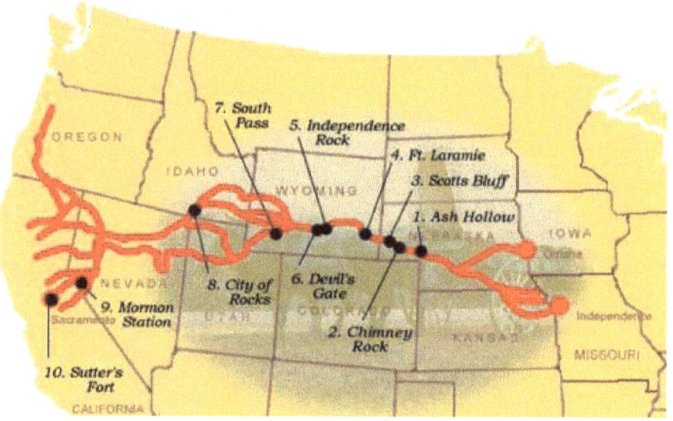

EMIGRANT TRAIN—GOLD HUNTERS 1849.

On January 24, 1848 - only 9 days before California was added to the American republic - gold was discovered at Sutter's Mill near Coloma, California. Thousands of people headed for California. Few discovered gold but they stayed to farm or start businesses. Cites grew along the route to California too and more states entered the union.

The rush to get west and be able to claim a fortune in gold encouraged the growth of stagecoach and wagon transportation. The most common starting point for the journey west was Independence, Missouri. The journey usually began in late April, early May. Often times there were huge jam ups as everyone wanted to leave at the same time. Often wagons were overloaded and the trails were littered with debris.

FREE LAND

In 1828, Congress designated the land that would become Oklahoma as Indian Territory. White settlers were required to leave, and a number of tribes from the East and South were forcibly moved into the area from their ancestral lands. Among these were the Five Civilized Tribes - the Cherokee, Choctaw, Chickasaw, Creek, and Seminole - who allied themselves with the South during the Civil War. Following the war, the U.S. Government looked upon these tribes as defeated enemies. This animosity combined with increasing pressure to open up the Indian Territory to white settlement prompted the Oklahoma land rush.

At precisely twelve noon on September 16, 1893 a cannon's boom unleashed the largest land rush America ever saw. Carried by all kinds of transportation - horses, wagons, trains, bicycles or on foot - an estimated 100,000 people raced to claim plots of land in northern Oklahoma Territory known as the Cherokee Strip. There had been a number of previous land rushes in the Territory but this was the most famous of them all.

By the time of the Oklahoma land rush of 1893, America was in the grip of the worst economic depression it had ever experienced. This was one of the factors that swelled the number of expectant land-seekers that day, but many would be disappointed. There were only 42,000 parcels of land available - far too few to satisfy the hopes of all those who raced for land that day. Additionally, many of the "Boomers" - those who had waited for the cannon's boom before rushing into the land claim - found that a number of the choice plots had already been claimed by "Sooners" who had snuck into the land claim area before the race began. The impact of the land rush was immediate, transforming the land almost overnight. (cited from: http://www.eyewitnesstohistory.com/landrush.htm)

INCHING WESTWARD

In the East there was no need for supply outposts. Towns were close together and people traveled from settlement to settlement by foot, horseback, cart or wagon. Eventually, roads were developed to connect these towns and settlements. Well known roads east of the Mississippi were the Coastal Road, Pennsylvania Pike, Genesee Road, National Road and Natches Trace.

As people moved westward, towns were further apart and transportation became challenging. There needed to be a way to get supplies from the east to the west, and then back to the east. Supply outposts were created and roads and canals were built to transport people and supplies.

Canals were waterways through the wilderness. The Erie Canal was built to bring trade from what was the American West back to the Port of New York. Originally, it ran 363 miles from where Albany meets the Hudson River to where Buffalo meets Lake Erie. The entire canal opened in 1825 and cut transport costs into, what was then, the wilderness by about 95%. It resulted in a massive population surge in western New York, opened regions further west to increased settlement, and was a prime factor in the growth of New York City as a port of trade. Canal channels were 4 to 5 feet deep and mostly mules pulled the flat bottom scows up and down the canal. Between 1825 and 1900, hundreds of thousands of mules labored on the canal towpaths.

ON YOUR MARK...GET SET...

St. Louis, one of the oldest cities in Missouri, began in 1763 when a man named Pierre Laclede Liguest discovered it to be the perfect place for a trading post on a high bluff of the Mississippi River. He named it St. Louis after Louis IX of France.

It was from St. Louis that Lewis and Clark started their journey west. The city became the "Gateway to the West" for the many mountain men, adventurers, and settlers that followed the path of Lewis and Clark into the new frontier.

St. Louis was the westernmost point in the United States accessible by rail until after the American Civil War. The existing mercantile network in St. Louis became firmly established by outfitting fortune-seekers. The city saw prosperity outfitting many a wagon train, trapper, miner, and trader along with operating more than 100 breweries in the city; the largest brewer, Anheuser-Busch, continues to maintain its world headquarters in St. Louis to this day.

At the time of the 1870 census St. Louis was the fourth largest city in the country. By 1890, the U.S. Census declared that the frontier had closed and America held no more unexplored and undiscovered lands. After this declaration, St. Louis grew at a more leisurely pace.

St. Louis was indeed the "Gateway to the West" it was where the journey to the west began - wagons were outfitted and it was time to...GO!

Steamboats and freight wagons crowd the
St. Louis landing 1853
(from Missouri History Museum)

GO!

Vast unsettled land between the east and west was only known to the early explorers and Native Americans. Routes to the west and outposts for supplies needed to be developed.

People could travel to the west from the east by land or sea. Sea travel was expensive and took about a year. Overland travel was cheaper. The 2,000 mile trip took 4 to 6 months. Passage averaged 15 to 20 miles on a good day. There were several trails that headed to the west.

The Oregon Trail was 2,000 miles and originated from Independence, Missouri and ended in Willamette Valley, Oregon. It was used by Native Americans, Lewis and Clark, fur traders, mountain men, and finally migrants.

The Santa Fe Trail began as a trade route. It was 800 miles from Independence, Missouri to Santa Fe, capital of Spanish New Mexico.

The Mormon Trail was 1,300 miles and started in Nauvoo, Illinois and ended in Salt Lake City. 16,000 Mormons migrated west on this trail between 1847 and 1853.

Central Overland Route used by Pony Express which was also known as, "Simpson's Route," or the "Egan Trail," was a transportation route from Salt Lake City, Utah south of the Great Salt Lake through the mountains of central Nevada to Carson City, Nevada. Pony Express was the fastest mail service crossing the Great Plains, the Rocky Mountains, and the High Sierras from St. Joseph, Missouri, to Sacramento, California from April 3, 1860 to October 1861.

Butterfield Overland Mail was a route also known as the Oxbow Route because of its long curving route through the southwest. It was 600 miles longer than the Central Overland Trail, but had the advantage of being snow free.

The Southern Route started at Fort Smith, Arkansas. It traveled south through New Mexico and Arizona then headed north into California, ending in San Francisco.

Old Spanish Trail connected the northern New Mexico settlements near Santa Fe, New Mexico with those of Los Angeles, California, and southern California.

The Oregon Trail was the oldest of the northern commercial and emigrant trails and was originally discovered and used by fur trappers and traders in the fur trade from about 1811 to 1840. This 2,000 mile historic east-west route connected various towns on the Missouri River to valleys in Oregon and locations in between.

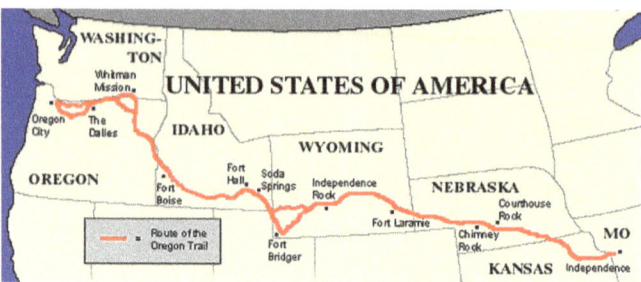

The Santa Fe Trail was at first an international trade route between the United States and Mexico. It was the 1846 U.S. invasion route of New Mexico during the Mexican–American War. The Santa Fe Trail sometimes had wagons traveling four a breast!

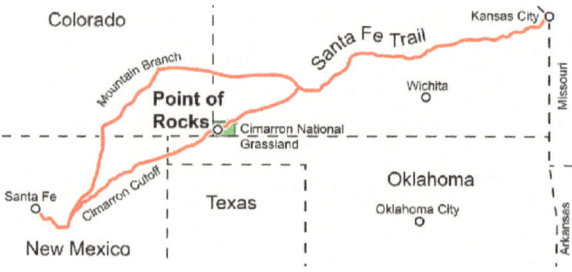

The Donner Party, a group of ill-fated pioneers, traveled through the Great Salt Lake Valley a year before the Mormon pioneers. In 1846, Brigham Young led the Latter-day Saints west into the territory owned by the Republic of Mexico after the death of their church founder, Joseph Smith, Jr. The PEF (Perpetual Emigration Fund) helped Mormon converts travel by wagon train across the Great Plains to Salt Lake City. In September 1855, with declining money and material available for the PEF, Brigham Young fell back on an old plan to make handcarts and let the emigration foot it. Despite the disastrous crossings, that were the worst single tragedies to befall any overland travelers, the church continued to support the handcart scheme. The Mormons of Salt Lake were an essential link between the east and west.

In 1857, Congress authorized the Postmaster General to contract for mail service from Missouri to California to facilitate settlement in the west. The Post Office Department advertised for bids for an overland mail service. Bidders were to propose routes from the Mississippi River westward. 9 bids were made by some of the most experienced stage men. None of the existing express companies, such as American Express, Adams Express or Wells Fargo and Company, bid on the contract because they had no experience running stage lines. The contract was given to John Butterfield of Utica, New York, who was president for the contract that was named the Overland Mail Company. The route he proposed was the route, known as the Oxbow Route, because of its long curving route through the southwest. It was 600 miles longer than the Central Overland Trail, but had the advantage of being snow free. The route went from Memphis, Tennessee and Saint Louis to merge at Fort Smith, Arkansas. It was also called the Southern Route since it traveled south through New Mexico and Arizona before heading north through California, ending in San Francisco.(cited from: https://en.wikipedia.org/wiki/Butterfield_Overland_Mail)

In 1860, the Pony Express was founded by William H. Russell, Alexander Majors and William B. Waddell. It was the fastest mail service to the west. Hannibal and St. Joseph Railroad was used to deliver mail to the Pony Express at St Joseph then the Pony Express used the Central Overland Route to get to California. This route traveled across Utah and Nevada for part of their fast 10 day mail delivery from St. Joseph, Missouri to Sacramento, California. In 1861, soon after the completion of the First Transcontinental Telegraph, the Pony Express was discontinued as the Transcontinental Telegraph now could provide quicker and cheaper communication from the East to the West. In 1861 John Butterfield, who since 1858, had been using the Butterfield Overland Mail route through the deserts of the American Southwest, also switched to the Central Route to avoid possible hostilities during the American Civil War. From 1862 to 1865 Wells Fargo operated a private express line between San Francisco and Virginia City, Nevada; Overland Mail stagecoaches covered the route from Carson City, Nevada, to Salt Lake City; and Ben Holladay, who had acquired the business of Russell, Majors & Waddell, ran a stagecoach line from Salt Lake City to Missouri.

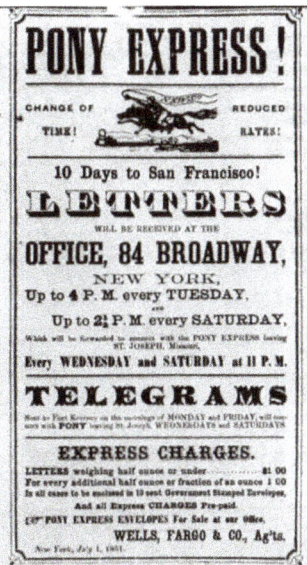

WESTWARD HO!

THE NEEDS

Stopping points and assembly points en route to destinations needed to be established to support the needs of the animals and passengers in route to the West. At the peak of westward expansion there were 841 horses, 7,547 mules, 67,950 oxen and 6,922 wagons servicing the freight needs of the Westward expansion in just one year. Freight wagons were essential to take hay, grain, supplies, and food to these staging areas and to the newly established towns. There was also a need for getting information from the East to the West.

The Butterfield Line, named for its president, John Butterfield, established twice-weekly mail and passenger service between St. Louis and San Francisco. Wells Fargo joined other express companies to finance the Overland Mail Company. The Butterfield Overland Mail Company traveled the 2,800 miles of the Oxbow Route in 25 days. Butterfield was paid $600,000 annually and had to outfit 160 stations, have 200 coaches and 200,000 horses. A passenger ticket cost $200 that would be equivalent to about $6,000 today! The coach rolled night and day with routine stops to change horses and have quick meals of coffee, jerky and biscuits.

In 1869, the First Transcontinental Railroad was completed using the level route along the Humboldt River to the north along much of the original California Trail route. Alongside the railroad, a telegraph line was also constructed since it was easier to maintain and supply operators and relay stations along the established railroad route. When the Golden Spike formalized the transcontinental railroad in 1869, the Iron Horse quickly expanded in all directions.

After 1869 much of the stage and freight lines traffic was now carried cheaper and faster on the railroad but the packages, mail, and passengers still had to get to the train and then to their final destination from the train stations. Stagecoaches and freight wagons continued to roll in areas where the rails ended. The number of banking and express offices grew from 460 in 1871 to 3,500 at the turn of the century!

At first, there were just tent cities then towns developed with homes, businesses, and farms nearby. There was a need for supplies for building the new towns and a need for supplies for forging out a new life. Freight wagons transported bulk quantities of commercial goods, supplies, raw materials, and equipment over lengthy distances.

GETTING SUPPLIES AND PEOPLE TO THE WEST

Freight wagons were heavy four-wheeled vehicles pulled by animals that were used for transporting bulk quantities of commercial goods, supplies, raw materials, and equipment over lengthy distances. These wagons transported goods to the relay stations and towns west of the Mississippi.

Lighter duty wagons that were used for short distance hauling are not considered freight wagons. These light duty wagons were used on farms and for delivery of goods. Later, on trails to the West, Conestoga wagons were too heavy to be pulled such long distances so west-bound travelers turned instead to smaller covered wagons These wagons were known as pioneer wagons or prairie schooners to transport families and household goods to new homes.

Freight wagons can be divided into eastern and western types. The eastern types were used where the terrain was flatter and less rugged. The western types were used in the rugged mountain terrain.

Eastern Model Characteristics
- Cast iron skeins
- Removable spring seat
- Stiff tongue
- Double box

Western Model Characteristics
- Steel skeins
- Rigid mounted seat
- Drop tongue
- Heavy duty box
- Mountain brake
- Iron gear

The National Stagecoach and Freight Wagon Association classifies freight wagons as follows:

Commercial Freighters
- Conestoga
- Large business/express
- Drays • Heavier farm
- Tall-sided
- Ore
- Ice

Military Freighters
- Escort
- Pontoon
- Daugherty

COMMERCIAL FREIGHTERS

The Conestoga Wagon was a heavy, broad-wheeled covered wagon. It was large enough to transport loads up to 8 tons and was drawn by horses, mules or oxen. The classic Conestoga wagon with its bent wood bows, cloth cover, and downward curved wagon box had its origin in Southeastern Pennsylvania during the Colonial era as a farm and freight wagon. Later, on trails to the West, Conestoga wagons and other smaller covered wagons, known as pioneer wagons, were also used to transport families and household goods to new homes.

The Conestoga Horse (now extinct) was developed in the United States during the 18th and early 19th centuries for pulling the famous Conestoga wagons that were produced in Lancaster County, Pennsylvania. The Conestoga Valley was settled in the early 18th century. It is thought that horses owned by Samuel Gist (the man who imported the first Thoroughbred to America) and George Washington may have been used for breeding in the development of Conestoga horses.

CONESTOGA.

For purposes of protection and efficiency, traders and emigrants gathered their wagons into more or less organized caravans or wagon trains.

Beginning in 1842, settlers came in covered wagons each spring to Elm Grove Missouri, elected their captains, guides and other officers, and began the long trek westward via the Oregon Trail. By 1843, only one year later, more than 1,000 emigrants moved over the same route in many wagons, some of which reached the banks of the Columbia River. In 1843, the celebrated "cow column" emigrant party of about 1,000 persons brought most of its 120 wagons to arrive near the Columbia River; it was the first wagon train to reach Oregon Country.

Caravans, large and small, were traveling on all of the trails across the Great Plains. The number of wagons making the overland journey annually from 1843 to 1848 is difficult to determine with accuracy. One report, dated 23 June 1849, estimated that 5,516 wagons had passed Fort Kearney on the Platte River (in present-day Nebraska), bound for California or the Columbia Valley.

By 1865, trains 5 miles long were occasionally reported. An average caravan was composed of scores of giant prairie schooners, each capable of transporting between 4,000 and 7,000 pounds and drawn usually by 5 or 6 yoke of oxen.

The organization and daily routine of a wagon train depended on the danger expected from the Native American tribes into whose territory it had traveled, the terrain, and the size of the caravan. Horse-or mule-drawn wagons could make from 10-15 miles a day. At night the wagons were commonly drawn up in a circle or a square, end to end, so as to form a corral for at least the more valuable horses, mules, and cattle, as well as a fortress for the passengers. Indian thefts, buffalo herds, storms, and animal stampedes made life in the wagon camps treacherous.

Even after the completion of the Union Pacific-Central Pacific railway line in May 1869, caravan trade and travel persisted for a decade. (cited from: https://www.encyclopedia.com/history/united-states-and-canada/us-history/wagon-train)

There wasn't much room in the smaller wagons. On fair-weather nights, the women typically slept in the wagons and the men either underneath the wagons or around a fire. This particular family seems to be a bit better off than most. They had a nice chair, oil lamp, lots of clothing, and even a spinning wheel. However, the travelers soon discovered that excess weight and unnecessary items slowed them down and took up room that could be used for sleeping and keeping safe from bad weather. Most of the spinning wheels and big chairs got thrown out along the way. cited from: http://oldphotoarchive.com/stories/inside-a-pioneer-covered-wagon

A view of a group of pioneers on the Oregon Trail. You can tell this was relatively early in their trip - the canvases aren't yet dark and tattered.

Budwieser Clydesdale Six-horse Hitch and Beer Wagon, in front of the St. Louis Brewery in 1933

Hitch Wagons, sometimes called express wagons or show wagons, were widely used for light trucking. Companies took great pride in the hitch wagons bearing their business name and in the magnificent team of horses that pulled them.

The Dray Wagon was a heavy-duty freight wagon. It had smaller wheels than on other wagons, a flat level floor, no sides, low sides, or stake sides, and it was low to the ground. (cited from: http://www.stagecoachfreightwagon.org/NSFWA/vehicle_freightwagon.html)

The Heavy Farm Wagon had higher sides than a buckboard and a heavier running gear. They were the backbone of western transportation hauling produce and merchandise to frontier towns. The Farm Wagon's design was both simple and utilitarian, making it sturdy enough for heavy loads over rural roads and dependable enough for everyday use. Famous wagon makers of the era–ever proud of their craftsmanship and mindful of promoting the sale of products-couldn't resist the opportunity to add beautiful signage and detailing to this functional design. The original finishes and signage is what adds historic flavor and value to these distinctive vehicles. (cited from: http:// www.hansenwheel.com/store/wagons-carriages/ farm-wagons-freight-wagons.html)

The **Tall-sided Wagon** was a heavy-duty freight wagon. They were often used in wagon trains with a lead wagon followed by multiple trail wagons.

Ore Wagons were larger than an average freight wagon and built to withstand the extreme stresses when loaded with ore. These monstrous wagons carried as much as 18,000 pounds of ore and had 6 foot wheels!

Twenty Mule Team Wagon used to haul ore from Harmony Borax Works near Furnace Creek Death Valley National Park California. Lead is a water wagon.

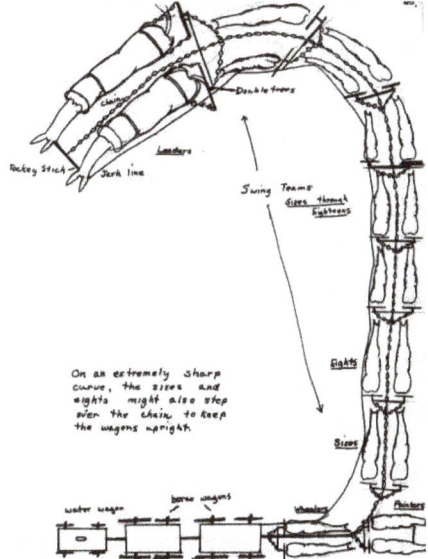

Twenty-mule Teams were teams of 18 mules and 2 horses attached to large wagons that transported borax out of Death Valley from 1883 to 1889. They traveled from mines across the Mojave Desert to the nearest railroad spur, 165 miles away in Mojave. 2 horses led the group. Though they were larger than the mules and had great strength for getting the wagons moving, they were not as well suited to the desert conditions as the mules. The 18 mules and 2 horses were latched to an 80-foot chain, which ran the length of the team. Although the driver also wielded a whip with a 6 foot handle and a 22-foot lash, his primary method of giving orders lay in manipulating this chain which was called the jerk line. Between 1883 and 1889, the 20 mule teams hauled more than 20 million pounds of borax out of the Valley. During those years, the teams ran like clockwork, completing the 330-mile round trip between the Harmony Borax Works and the railhead in about 20 days, despite the difficult terrain. (cited from: https://www.legendsofamerica.com/ca-20muleteams/)

Freight wagons, piled high with food and supplies, provided the life-blood for forts, pioneers and settlers. Teams from 10 to 20 mules or horses pulled them across the desert and mountains. These outfits, with a load capacity of 10 tons each, were usually operated by 2 men; the driver, riding the wheel horse would c ontrol the teams with a 'jerk line' to the lead horse, and the swamper, who would clamber from wagon to wagon, setting brakes.
(cited from: https://www. hansenwheel.com/resources/faqs-wagon-history/)

After gold was discovered in the Black Hills in 1874, there became a need to transport people and freight to the "Hills." One of the shortest and easiest travel routes was overland from Fort Pierre, South Dakota the nearest river landing, to Deadwood, the epicenter of gold mining. From 1874 to 1908, thousands of tons of freight and hundreds of people arrived in Fort Pierre by riverboat or railroad destined for Deadwood. From Fort Pierre the freight was loaded on wagons pulled by teams of draft aanimals. (cited from: https://www.fortpierre.com/attractions/norman-signs-fort-pierre-deadwood-trail/)

Deadwood Trail Freight-line

There were many ways one could get to Deadwood or the surrounding Black Hills. In fact, the hardest decision was not whether to go to the Black Hills, but which road to take. There were three options for freight and passengers: the trails to Deadwood from Cheyenne (Wyoming Territory), Sidney (Nebraska), and Bismarck and Fort Pierre (Dakota Territory). Travelers brave enough to test their luck on the wagon trails often were in for harsh surprises, including Indian attacks, water shortages, bogged out roads and robberies. For those lucky enough to make it to the Black Hills, the rewards often outweighed the struggles. For others, the Wild West would be their final resting place. (cited from: https://www.blackhillsknowledge-network.org/home/ the-many-trails-into-deadwood-helped-make-history.html)

Both horses and oxen pulled wagons, but oxen were the prime choice, for they were both sturdy and tough. Oxen could be expected to travel about 12 to 15 miles each day. Bullwhackers, as they were called, were the men who drove the oxen wagons. They got their name because they would use whips, also known as bullwhackers, to drive the oxen.
(cited from: https://www.blackhillsknowledgenetwork.org/home/the-many-trails-into-deadwood-helped-make-history.html)

Rapid City Freight Team

Mining was the main enterprise of Ketchum, Idaho. The first shipment of ore came out of the Elkhorn Mine in August 1880. The Lewis Fast Freight Line sent wagon trains from Ketchum out to mines in Clayton, Challis, Bayhorse, Custer and Bonanza in the 1880s and '90s. The Lewis Fast Freight Line took supplies out to the mines on a route over Trail Creek Summit called the Ketchum-Challis Toll Road. At its largest, the line had 30 wagon trains on the road at all times, constantly ferrying supplies out to the mines and hauling ore and silver bullion back to Ketchum. The freight line used as many as 700 horses and mules at its peak operation.

Trail Creek Freight Train - Mackay to Ketchum

True freight wagons had a board that slid out in front of the left back wheel on which the driver could sit or stand. Horse collars and harnesses were made for pulling, but there was no way the horses could hold a load back on the downhill. From the lazy board, the driver could work the brake handle which levered wood-blocks against the back wheel rims to brake on the downhill. Sometimes they would nail an old shoe sole in the groove of the brake wood-block as leather provided better friction than wood, hence the term: "brake shoe." On steep down-hills they could chain one back wheel fast to the wagon so it just slid. The rigs were called "Six Horse Bell Teams" because of the practice of having a bow with three or four brass bells suspended over each collar in the Russian manner, except on the wheel horse, which the teamster rode. The tinkling of 20 bells was a warning for all to get out of the way. When a wagon got "stumped" on a snag or stuck in mud, the next driver along would unhitch his team and help to free the mired wagon. The fee was a hoop of bells. Thus the origin of the phrase "to be there with 'bells on,'" meaning to arrive trouble free. (cited from: https://www.berksmontnews.com/opinion/thehistorian-six-horse-bell-teams/article_d18af4c7-05d4-5c32-a7af-89ed696e452f.html)

Conestoga horses with bells

MILITARY FREIGHTERS

During the American Revolutionary War, the Continental Armies used nearly every means of wagon transportation at their disposal. One of the most commonly used wagons was the Conestoga wagon, designed for heavy loads of supplies. The development of the Army Escort Wagon was in response to the need to transport supplies and troops in a more organized fashion. The military escort wagon was a heavy-duty freight wagon used by the military.  Studebaker, Kentucky, Thornhill and International Harvester had government contracts to build wagons for the military. At the end of the Civil War, nearly 6000 wagons were in storage at the Quartermaster depot in Washington, DC. Many of these were shipped to Fort Leavenworth, Kansas to use at various military posts throughout the western frontier.

While many changes took place to the Six-Mule Wagon during its use, there were many constants. From the beginning, the wagon had a Venetian Red running gear with the body painted a "pure Prussian Blue on the exterior and Venetian Red on the interior." All ironwork was painted black. It wasn't until after the turn of the century that the Army switched these wagon colors for a dark olive green.

In 1875, a board of officers were directed to investigate the adoption of lighter weight "two-horse and fourhorse or mule wagons, for use in the Army." For economic reasons, the Army adopted a new lighter weight wagon, which would be less expensive to build, take fewer animals to pull and require less harness. 50 of these wagons were produced for testing and after field observations and reports, changes were made to the wagon design specifications and approved in November of 1878. (cited from: https://www.hansenwheel.com/history-of-the-army-wagon)

Early in 1864, the commander of the Army of the Cumberland, Major General George H. Thomas, was seeking a light-weight, easy-to-haul and erect pontoon bridge to move his troops across unfordable rivers and streams. Knowing the limitations of the two systems used by the armies in the Western Theater, he had folding pontoons developed. The new design yielded a portable boat that was lightweight, small enough to carry on a standard supply wagon, and easier to construct in the field. It was also strong enough to support horse-drawn artillery and fully loaded wagons. (cited from: https://en.wikipedia.org/wiki/Cumberland_Pontoons)

Pontoon wagon A single pontoon was mounted upon a wagon frame. The pontoon boat's cable and anchor were placed inside the boat. The oars, rowlocks, boathooks and ropes were lashed under the rear axle. This wagon required that 6 horses be hitched to it due to its weight. In order that the horses not be overtaxed, the boat and its accouterments were all that was allowed to be carried within or upon this wagon.

The Chess Wagon This wagon ould be loaded one way only. The chess planks were loaded tightly together vertically with 2 layers consisting of 20 planks to each layer. Above the first layer, 5 planks were laid horizontally and another vertical row of 20 planks were laid on top of them. The chess wagon also carried 2 cables and was drawn by 6 horses.

The Tool Wagons This specific wagon would carry all the other necessary items for the construction of the bridge and the abutments. These wagons carried the entrenching tools, spare cordage, bridge hardware and carpenter's tools. The forge wagons would carry extra iron for the bridge and anchors and would help care for the horses and mules. This entire bridge train would be followed by its own supply train.(cited from: http://www.wadehamptoncamp.org/pontoon.html)

Pontoon Boats on Wagons

Chess Wagon

Originating in St. Louis, Dougherty Wagons were used throughout the early days of the American frontier and into the 20th century. There were slight changes in the ultra-nimble design over the years including a raised driver's seat and cut-under body for tighter turning. Most nineteenth century Dougherty wagons were equipped with a set of elliptical springs balancing all 4 corners of the body. They featured doors on both sides, canvas curtains that could be raised and lowered, and a luggage rack in the rear. The design was also referred to as an ambulance and was often used to transport officers and their families as well as paymasters and other special needs related to military business.

In 1911, L. Mervin Maus, a Colonel in the U.S. Army reminisced about his past experiences with the wagon…

"Anyone who has failed to travel in a Dougherty wagon has never enjoyed one of the real pleasures of life and one of the genuine refinements of wheel transportation. He has missed something which has left a hiatus in his life and a blank that can never be filled until he finds himself at last safely seated in one of these classical army chariots, behind four snappy, faithful, and patriotic government mules, such as for generations have been the friend of the army at frontier posts and his ally in conducting campaigns."
(cited from: http://wheelsthat-wonthewest.blogspot-com/2016/12/hard-to-find-vehi-cles.html)

Zouave ambulance crew demonstrating removal of wounded soldiers from the field

The nation's first ambulance corps, organized to rush wounded soldiers to battlefront hospitals and using wagons, developed and deployed for that purpose, was created during the Civil War. The idea was to collect wounded soldiers from the field, take them to a dressing station and then transport them to the field hospital. (cited from: https://www.aarp.org/politics-society/history/info-04-2011/8-ways-civil-war-changed-lives.html)

On more than one occasion, General Dwight D. Eisenhower perplexed younger officers by referring to a Dougherty wagon. Having joined the military in 1911, "Ike" was well acquainted with a type of wagon frequently used as an ambulance. Around the time of the Civil War, such wagons were made in St. Louis by a man named Dougherty. (cited from: https://helenair.com/lifestyles/crosscut/the-diary-of-a-civil-war-era-ambulance/article_ff97df94-3151-550c-9d3f-7bb587b10050.html)

GETTING AROUND IN THE WEST

Stagecoaches were used from eastern Maine to San Diego to transport, passengers, mail, currency and gold. Coaches were various sizes and built to carry either six, nine, or twelve passengers.

In 1869, the Transcontinental Railroad was completed but railroads actually did NOT destroy the stage lines. Vehicles were used around the railroad heads to take people and parcels to their final destination. Over 40 different types of vehicles, including 3,000 Concord coaches were used. Wells Fargo Stagecoaches carried news, mail and passengers where trains did not go. From Salt Lake City, passengers boarded stagecoaches to travel 400 miles to Boise, Idaho and 700 miles to Fort Benton, Montana. From Salt Lake City, Wells Fargo stagecoaches connected with trains east in Nebraska.

A shipment of 30 Abbott and Downing coaches to the west.

Wells Fargo began when prosperous New York businessmen, Henry Wells, and William Fargo saw great opportunity in the west after gold was discovered. The pair, who had helped to found American Express in 1850, officially created Wells Fargo & Co. on March 18, 1852, with two primary objectives – transportation and banking.

By 1855, mining activity had begun to decline in California and several banks failed. However, Wells Fargo remained, soon to become the dominant express and banking organization in the west. At that time, they were the only company making large shipments of gold and continued to serve miners by delivering mail and supplies. In 1857, Wells Fargo helped back the new Overland Mail Company, which provided for regular twicea-week mail service between St. Louis and San Francisco. Wells Fargo would still often use its own wagons and guards, as the Overland Mail Company forbid the shipment of any valuables.

When the Civil War broke out, the route changed, moving northward across the Great Plains and over the Rocky Mountains, before snaking its way to California.

In 1866, Wells Fargo expanded its operations again, buying, what was then, Ben Holladay's Overland Mail Express, and consolidating all the other independent companies on what was known as the "Central Route", to create the largest stagecoach company in the world. They controlled virtually all the stage lines from Mississippi to California. It was 1867 when Wells Fargo finally achieved the total running of a stage line with its logo actually on the side of a stagecoach. They placed their first order for 30 Concord stagecoaches with Abbot-Downing & Company on April 20, 1867.

During these fast and furious stagecoach heydays, Wells Fargo also became the primary focus of bandits and thieves. By the turn of the century, Wells Fargo had more than 3,000 offices in nearly every state and in Mexico. Wells Fargo was told to "throw down the box" from a Concord stage for the last time in 1908. The bandits were immediately pursued, this time in automotive vehicles. The last horse-drawn stage carrying Wells Fargo cargo ran between Tonopah and Manhattan, Nevada, in 1909. Today, Wells Fargo & Co. provides financial services at some 6,000 locations. (cited from: https://www.legendsofamerica.com/wells-fargo/)

A STAGECOACH FOR EVERY PURPOSE

The kinds of stages depended largely upon the character and the condition of the roads, the distances to be traveled and their urban or rural destinations. Manufacturers produced many different styles in various sizes for stage travel. They ranged from classic overland coaches to open-sided wagons, including celerity wagons and mud wagons, mountain wagons and Yosemite coaches. On the roughest Western roads, the Butterfield Overland Mail and later Wells, Fargo & Co. frequently transferred passengers and mail to lightweight, more durable celerity wagons or to the less expensive, but also light mud wagons. (cited from: https://www.parks.ca.gov /?page_id=25449)

Stagecoaches can be divided into eastern and western designs. The eastern types were used where the terrain was flatter and less rugged. The western types were used in the rugged mountain terrain. Eastern Stagecoaches include: Eastern Concord Stagecoach, Eastern Mud Wagon and the Eastern Mountain Wagon. Western Stagecoaches include: Western Concord Stagecoach, Western Mud Wagon, Yosemite Wagon, and the Western Mountain Wagon.

Western Model Characteristics

- Flexible leather bag boot
- Leather covered rear boot on flexible frame
- Two to three bunters
- Pad on the brake served as a coach step
- Coach lamps were designed to invert the glass frame
- Heavy ¾" thick iron tires
- Axle mounted on top of reach
- Doubletree
- Albany bed plate

Eastern Model Characteristics

- Rigid front box boot
- Rigid open rear luggage rack
- Single front bunter
- Folding coach step
- Rear axle mounted beneath reaches
- Kingpin in front of axle
- Splinter bar
- Standard casto

MUD WAGON

One of the most common and preferred stage vehicles used in the West by stage operators was the mud wagon. Unlike the classic Concord stagecoaches, which could be mired in bad weather, mud wagons—true to their name—could travel over trails and roads during inclement weather. However, the only protection provided for passengers against bad weather and dusty roads were the canvas side-curtains, which could be rolled down and fastened. It was tough and durable, but lighter in weight than a Concord stagecoach and had a lower center of gravity, making it good for mountain roads, such as those routinely servicing mining camps. (cited from: https://www.parks.ca.gov/?page_id=25449)

Sometimes called a stage wagon, the mud wagon had a more complex design than the mountain wagon but was simpler than the Concord stagecoach. It was mostly used as a passenger wagon and was designed to be light weight. It was used in mountainous regions with poor roads. The name "mud wagon" comes from the fact that the roads it was used on were often muddy.

Manufacturers

- Abbot-Downing
- M.P. Henderson

Characteristics

- Light weight design
- Exterior framing
- Iron rockers
- Leather thorough braces
- Canvas storm curtains

CELERITY WAGON

The innovative design for the celerity wagon is attributed to John Butterfield. Instead of having a heavy wooden top, typical of most coaches, it had a light frame structure with a thick duck or canvas covering. This reduced the weight of the vehicle. Its wheels were also set further apart and were protected by wide steel rims. These details helped to keep the vehicle from tipping over or the wheels from sinking in soft roadside sands. While not as comfortable for daytime travelers as the larger, well-appointed overland coaches, they were designed for passenger travel at night. Abbot and Downing's version of the celerity wagon used thorough braces which made the ride more comfortable for passengers and far safer for the animals pulling the vehicle. It also was smaller, having two passenger seats. It was more maneuverable on mountain roads and across deserts. It could carry 500 to 600 pounds of mail. Because of the light roof construction, baggage was stowed in the boot at the back of the vehicle or, if need be, inside with the passengers, but not on top. Wide window and door openings also kept the celerity wagon lightweight, letting the air flow through along with the dust and the rain. Heavy duck or leather roll-down curtains were the passengers' only protection from the elements. (cited from: https://www.parks.ca.gov/?page_id=25449)

MOUNTAIN WAGON

The mountain wagon was also a type of stagecoach. It had the simplest design of all the stagecoach designs. It was mostly used as a passenger wagon in mountainous regions of the far West from the mid 1800's to the early 1900's.

Manufacturers

- Studebaker

Characteristics

- Three reaches
- Side springs
- Elliptical cross springs
- Two to Four seats positioned crosswise
- High standing top
- Luggage rack
- Roll down curtains for protection

Mountain wagons are sometimes called platform wagons. They were used for short trips, perhaps from a rail depot into town or between two adjacent communities. Alzada, Montana is in the far southeastern corner of the state and far from any other community, so this coach was probably used in town. The front passenger is actually sitting in the driver's seat; the seating capacity of this vehicle is not very large.

OBSERVATION WAGON

Some coaches were custom built by the Abbot-Downing Company specifically for touring national parks. Since you came for sightseeing, Yellowstone stagecoaches were all ordered with the seats facing forward and open sides rather than enclosed cabs so that you could see the scenery. Some of the most notable models were the 6 horse "Tally-Ho" stagecoaches, which transported guests from the train depot stationed at Gardiner, Montana, over the 5 miles to the Mammoth Hot Springs Hotel. "Tally Ho" stagecoaches featured 4 interior seats, as well as an exterior rear seat, and even hosted seats on the roof. From the Mammoth Hotel, guests loaded onto smaller, Yellowstone Observation Wagons, which were pulled by 4 horses. These coaches were used to take 10 visitors per coach on the "Grand Loop" tour, where they would ride together for 5 days viewing the various sites throughout the park. (cited from: /www.yellowstonenationalparklodges.com/connect/yellowstone-hot-spot/stagecoaches-in-yellowstone/)

Yellowstone Observation Wagon

Tally Ho

TRANSFER OMNIBUS

In larger cities, omnibuses and wagonettes, the two generic terms for wagons designed to transport groups of people, tended to be plush and sophisticated. Omnibuses usually had either curtains or glass windows to protect passengers from inclement weather and could seat up to 14 passengers plus standees. Some omnibuses even had a second level of seating on the roof of the vehicle. (cited from: https://nationalcowboymuseum.org/explore/hoofs-wheels-transportation-west/)

Often graced with elaborate lettering and ornamentation, these large, early 'buses' were built in different sizes. Many were designed for around a dozen passengers while, perhaps, the largest one in America measured 36 feet long and was reported to have a capacity of 120 passengers. Advertising messages for businesses eventually found their way onto many of these vehicles – just as buses and city cabs still incorporate today. Andrew Wight was a notable builder of omnibuses as well as street cars, express business, and freight wagons, and also circus wagons and cages. (cited from: http://wheelsthatwonthewest.blogspot.com/2017/05/an-omnibus-overview.html)

Omnibus built by Andrew Wight.

CONCORD COACH

The Concord coach was the most complex design of all stagecoaches. Concord, New Hampshire served as the center for coach production. It began when wheelwright Lewis Downing, whose shop opened in 1813, joined his skills with expert coach builder J. Stephens Abbot from Maine. Together they took stagecoach construction to a new level. In 1826, the two began turning out their first coaches. The partnership lasted over 20 years, turning into a thriving, world-renowned business. What separated Abbot and Downing from other coach builders of their day were the vehicles' handsome appearance, durability, and overall quality. These masterpieces of construction had no equal. Concord stages were first to offer shock-absorbing thorough braces—an important feature not just for passengers, but for the animals pulling them, too. (cited from: https:// www.parks.ca.gov/?page_id=25449)

Manufacturers
• Abbot-Downing

Characteristics
• Leather thorough braces

STAGECOACH TRAVEL – GOOD TO KNOW!

- The best seat inside a stagecoach is the one next to the driver. You will have to ride with your back to the horses, which with some people produces an illness not unlike seasickness, but in a long journey this will wear off, and you will get more rest with less than half the bumps and jars than on any other seat. When anyone who traveled thousands of miles on coaches offers, through sympathy, to exchange his back or middle seat with you, don't do it.

- Bathe your feet before starting in cold weather and wear loose overshoes and gloves two or three sizes too large.

- When the driver asks you to get off and walk, do it without grumbling. He will not request it unless absolutely necessary.

- If a team runs away, sit still and take your chances; if you jump, nine times out of ten you will be hurt.

- In very cold weather abstain entirely from liquor while on the road; a man will freeze twice as quick while under its influence.

- Don't growl at food at stations; stage companies generally provide the best they can get.

- Don't keep the stage waiting; many a virtuous man has lost his character by so doing.

- Don't smoke a strong pipe inside especially early in the morning; spit on the leeward side of the coach.

- If you have anything to take in a bottle, pass it around; a man who drinks by himself in such a case is lost to all human feeling.

- Provide stimulants before starting; ranch whiskey is not always nectar.

- Be sure and take two heavy blankets with you; you will need them.

- Don't swear, nor lop over onto your neighbor when sleeping.

- Don't ask how far it is to the next station until you get there.

- Take small change to pay expenses.

- Never attempt to fire a gun or pistol while on the road; it may frighten the team and the careless handling and cocking of the weapon makes people nervous.

- Don't discuss politics or religion, nor point out places on the road where horrible murders have been committed, if delicate women are among the passengers.

- Don't linger too long at the pewter washbasin at the station.

- Don't grease your hair before starting or dust will stick there in sufficient quantities to make a respectable "tater" patch.

- Tie a silk handkerchief around your neck to keep out dust and prevent sunburns.

- Don't imagine for a moment you are going on a picnic; expect annoyance, discomfort and some hard ships.

- If you are disappointed, thank heaven.

(cited from: the New Hampshire Historical Society attributed to the Omaha Herald, 1877)

Stagecoach Signage advertising routes and rates.

Stages leaving Bartlett Springs.

ABBOTT AND DOWNING

Lewis Downing, a wheelwright, started a wagon building business in Concord, New Hampshire on August 3, 1813. By 1826, seeing the need for road type coaches, and needing the services of an expert coach body builder, Downing engaged the services of J. Stephens Abbot and the men entered into partnership in the next year.

In 1873 they formed a corporation under the name "Abbott-Downing Company". Abbot and Downing was the premier builder of stagecoaches. They stayed in business as late as 1925. In 1945 the corporate name was sold to Wells Fargo.

Abbot and Downing became known all over the world for its "Concord Stagecoach". However, the company actually manufactured over 40 different types of carriages and wagons at their wagon factory in Concord, New Hampshire. The Concord Stagecoaches were built as solid as the Abbot and Downing Company's reputation and became known as coaches that didn't break down. Each coach was given a number by the Abbot-Downing factory, and each has its own story.

Lewis Downing

J. Stephens Abbott

John Burgum joined the company in 1850 to paint landscapes, figures and floral images. Hotels often had names on the coaches also. John's first work for the Abbot and Downing Coach company was the decoration of a circus wagon, but it was the famous Concord Coaches, exported all over the world, that made the company, and John, such a success.

The Concord Coaches had a reputation for being sturdy, roomy, and comfortable. The mid-1800s definitions of "roomy" and "comfortable" were far different from today's definitions!

In 1880, John Pleasant Gray recorded after traveling from Tucson to Tombstone: "That day's stage ride will always live in my memory – but not for its beauty spots. Jammed like sardines on the hard seats of an old time leather spring coach – a Concord – leaving Pantano, creeping much of the way, letting the horses walk, through miles of alkali dust that the wheels rolled up in thick clouds of which we received the full benefit ... It is always a mystery to the passenger how many can be wedged into and on top of a stagecoach. If it had not been for the long stretches when the horses had to walk, enabling most of us to get out and "foot it" as a relaxation, it seems as if we could never have survived the trip." (cited from: https://en.wikipedia.org/wiki/Stagecoach)

Most of the time, the Abbot and Downing Company employed about 300 people. All were men except for one: from 1865 to 1895 Marie F. Putnam stitched leather seats and trim for every stagecoach that rolled out of the Concord factory, including those purchased by Wells Fargo & Company. For the entire 30 years, she was the company's only female employee.

Marie F. Putnam

THE DEADWOOD COACH

Perhaps the most historic Concord stagecoach in existence is the famous Deadwood coach, which was carried for many years by Buffalo Bill in his Wild West shows all over America and Europe. This coach was built by the Abbott-Downing Company, of Concord, New Hampshire, in 1863. This coach, in company with many others, was shipped to San Francisco, via Cape Horn, in 1864, and was used for many years in the mountains of California.

Eventually, traveling the trails across the Rockies, it came into possession of the stage company operating in eastern Wyoming and the Black Hills. The stage was fitted up as a treasure-stage to carry the gold from Deadwood to the railroad. The Deadwood coach's first baptism came with the killing of a driver, John Slaughter, in the White Wood Canyon. He was filled with buckshot, but the teams ran away, and the coach arrived safely at Greeley Station, thus outwitting the bandits. From now on the coach went through several baptisms of fire, generally escaping without loss of life or treasure, until a drummer from Chicago was killed and a companion injured. The Indians also attempted on several occasions to hold up the stage, but were successfully repelled.

Bandits, by treachery, successfully staged the Cold Spring tragedy. The bandits first captured the station, making away with its keepers, and hid themselves, awaiting the arrival of the stage. Soon the stage arrived, and Jean Barnet, not suspecting danger, drew his teams to a standstill at the stable door. A crashing volley killed Hugh Stevenson and Gail Hill, and wounded the other guards, making resistance impossible. Over $60,000 in gold was secured by the outlaws. A little later the coach was again attacked. The first volley killed the driver, and just as the bandits felt sure of success, a woman, Martha Canary, who afterward became known as "Calamity Jane," who was riding on the seat with the driver, seized the lines, gave the whip to the team, and amid a running fire brought the coach safely into its destination.

Last trip of the Deadwood Stage

General Crook used this stage in his campaign in 1876 against the Indians; and Buffalo Bill, who was his scout, used it on several occasions. After the campaign Buffalo Bill learned that the coach had been abandoned during an Indian attack and was lying neglected, away out in the hostile country, so, with a few companions, he proceeded to rescue and bring it back to camp. The coach continued its daily trips on the Black Hills stage line until Buffalo Bill organized his Wild West shows.

Wells Fargo currently has 11 original Abbot & Downing stagecoaches in its care. 8 are proudly displayed in museums and exhibits. Wells Fargo has 12 museums in the United States.

He secured possession of the historic coach, using it to depict the drama of overland staging in the Wild West. Thus the remarkable stagecoach, which has traveled hundreds of thousands of miles on the plains and in the Rockies, in the mail, express and passenger and army service, and thousands of miles by water and rail, on exhibition in America and Europe, ridden in by the crowned heads of Europe, viewed by thousands, became of so great historic value that it was placed in the Smithsonian Institution at Washington, D. C., for preservation. Today, the coach is at the Buffalo Bill Historical Center, an affiliate of the Smithsonian Institution in Cody, Wyoming. (cited from: https://www.legendsofamerica.com/we-deadwoodstage/)

ANATOMY OF A STAGECOACH

Axle - Cross structure that wheels attach

Brake - Device used to apply pressure to wheels to slow or stop wagon

Boot - A luggage compartment

Front boot - Located at the front of the coach

Rear boot - Located at the rear of the coach

Driver's box - The seat upon which the driver sits

Chock log - A block used to stop wagons rolling backward when resting animals on steep uphill grades

Doubletree - A crossbar, pivoted at the middle, with a singletree attached at each end. Used for harnessing horses side-by-side

Stiff Tongue - Rigid

Drag shoe - Device used to slow wagons on downhill grades

Reach - Structure that connects the front and rear axles

Rough Locks - Chains used to lock wheels. Used when resting animals on steep uphill grades

Singletree - A crossbar, pivoted at the middle, to which the traces of a harness are fastened (Also known as a whiffletree, whippletree, or swingletree)

Skeins - The metal spindle that attaches to the ends of a wooden axle on which the wheel box rests.

Springs - Steel structure that suspended wagon body above the reach

Thorough brace - Leather straps that suspend the coach body above the reach

Tongue - Device that attaches to front axle of vehicle

Drop Tongue - Hinged in the rear

Wheel - A circular ring designed to rotate around the axle

Box - The metal piece that fits inside the hub and slides over the skein

Hub - The center of the wheel

Spoke - The spindles of the wheel

Rim - The steel outermost part of the wheel

Stagecoach Parts

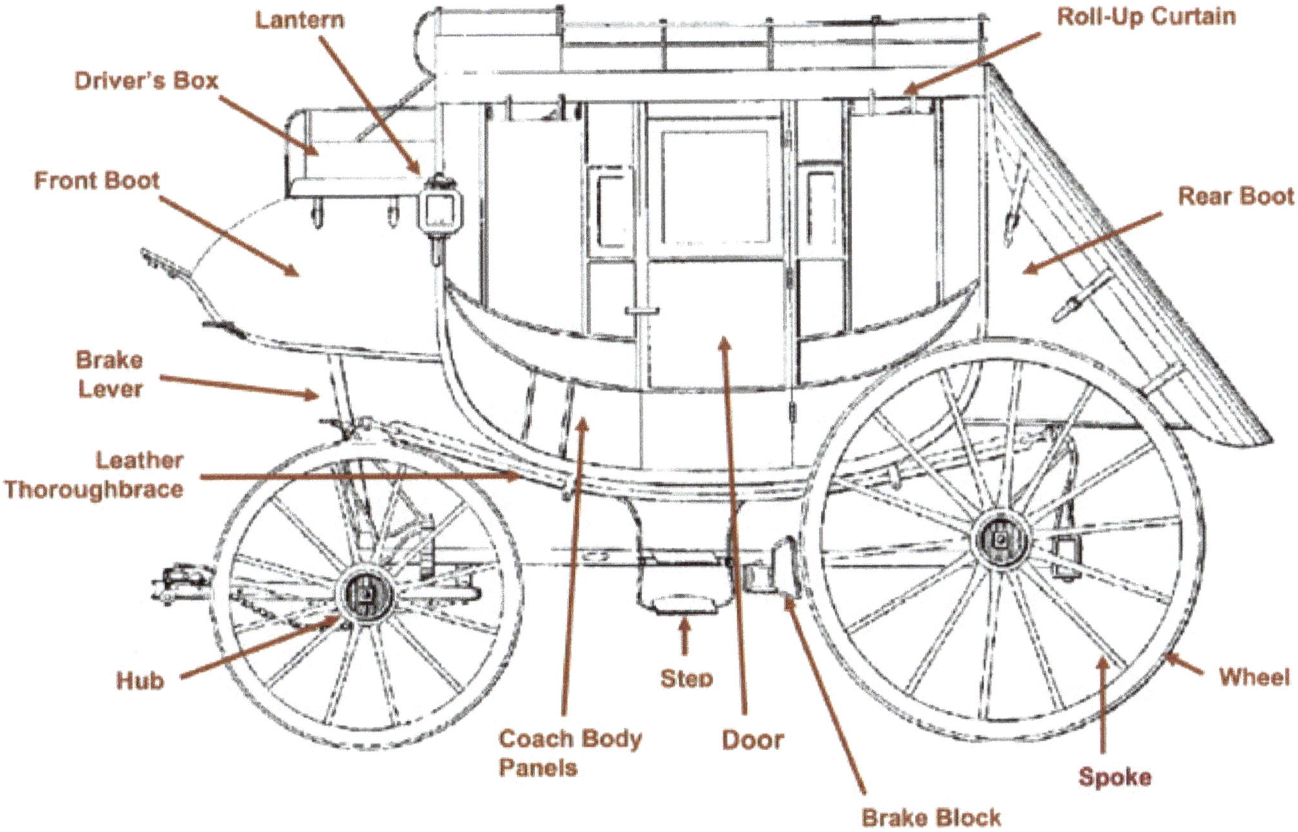

Undercarriage of Concord Coach
From Steffen, R. "Stagecoach!" Western Horseman, July, 1962.

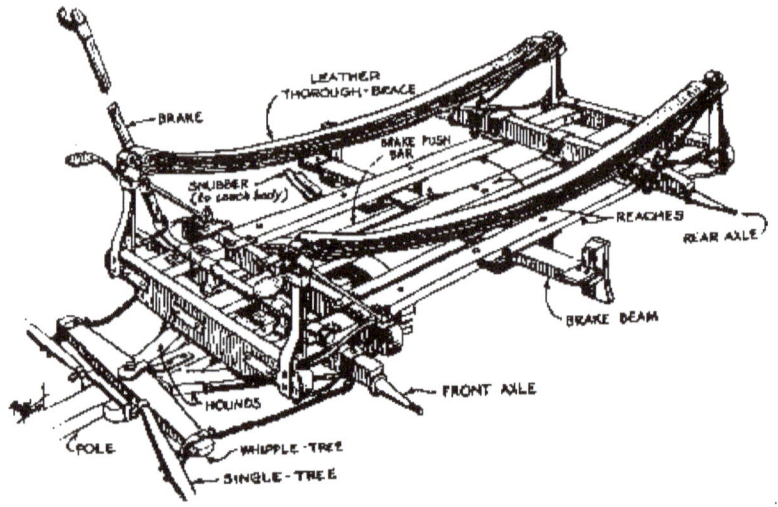

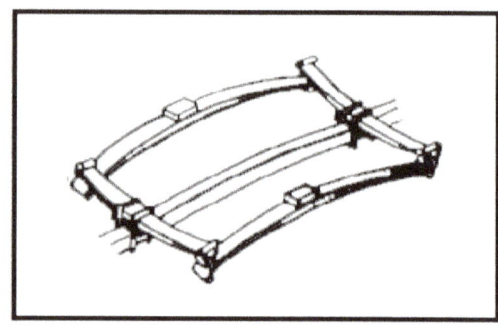

As opposed to a Telegraph Spring

The thoroughbrace suspension was key to the success of the Concord stagecoaches. It prevented the shock of the rough roads from transferring to the body. The use of a telegraph spring would have shaken the body apart on rough or in areas with no roads.

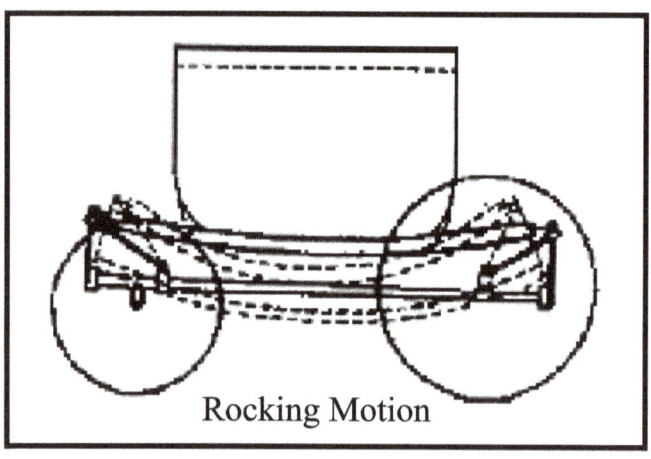

The egg-shaped body on the leather thoroughbrace system created a rocking motion. This saved the body from shaking apart but often caused passengers to become sick.

The Brake was not operated by the driver's hand, as was typical of the carriages of the time, but by the driver's foot.

Nothing much stopped the horses except shear exhaustion.

Since the body rocked to and fro, the brake often had to be applied in the turns to brace the driver enough to have contact with the horses' mouths.

The Guard on a stage coach served in several capacities: pebble man, gun wielder, and horn sounder.

As pebble man he lobed small stones at the leader of six which could not be reached by the drivers whip.

The guard "riding shotgun" shared the seat with the driver. The gun was used on thieves and varmints.

The bugle heralded the arrival in town and warned others to get out of the way – "the coach is coming through."

THE AUSTIN COACH

Willi Green of Orient, Ohio built this reproduction of an Eastern style Concord Coach for Gloria Austin. An Eastern hotel-type body has no leather boots. The roof top has one forward seat and a luggage rack rather than an extra seat. The Austin coach is painted in the Wells Fargo colors – straw and red. (Pictures on the following pages are close-up views of the Austin Coach.)

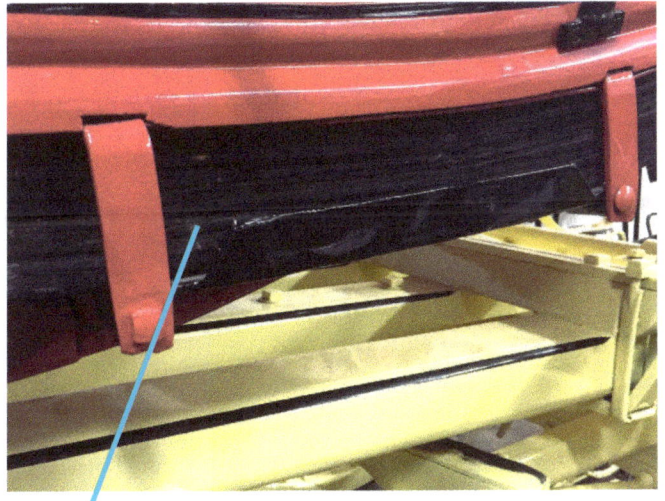

Thoroughbraces sit in a channel.

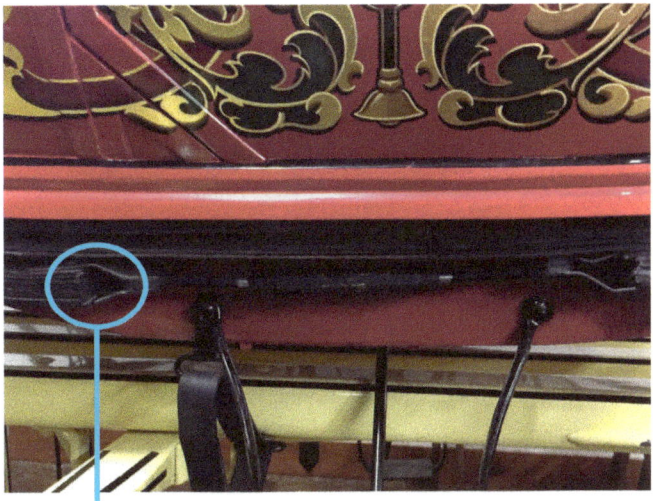

Turnbuckle for a thoroughbrace

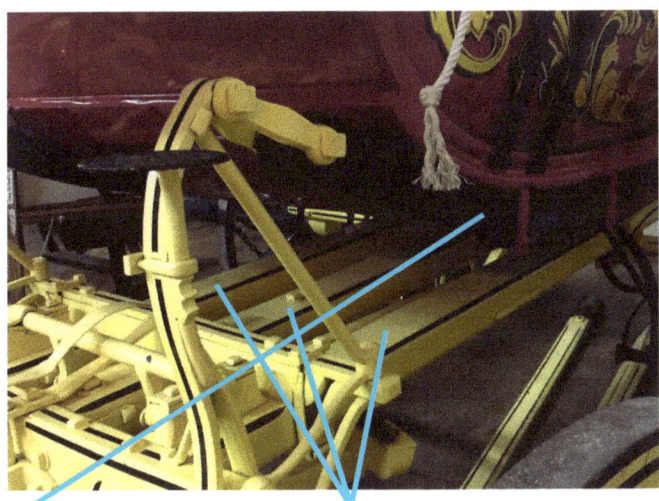

1. Thoroughbraces sit in a channel.
2. Concord coaches had 3 perches for extra strength.

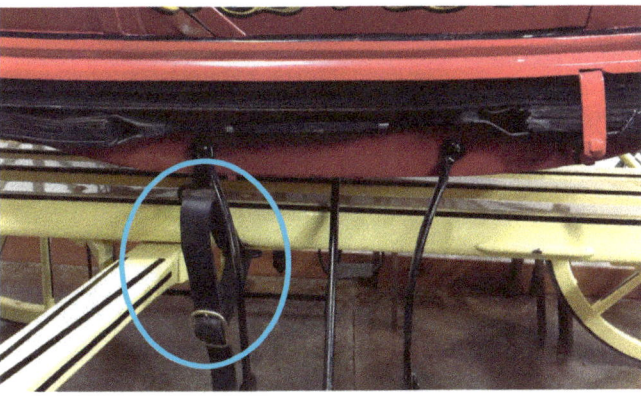

Leather sway strap

Wayne Troyer of Cleveland, Ohio did the art work on the Austin Concord Coach. On the original Concord Coaches, two different crews painted the bodies and gears. Murals were designs apropos to a particular area or theme. The designs on the Austin coach are scenes in Florida: palm trees, sailing and golf.

The Austin Coach was designed to seat 6 passengers, but it is still a tight squeeze.

The top of the coach is equipped to carry cargo. A leather boot covered the rear cargo space on Western Mail Coaches.

The center drop-away windows had leather curtains that could be rolled down for air but it was not long before dust would take over and cover all.

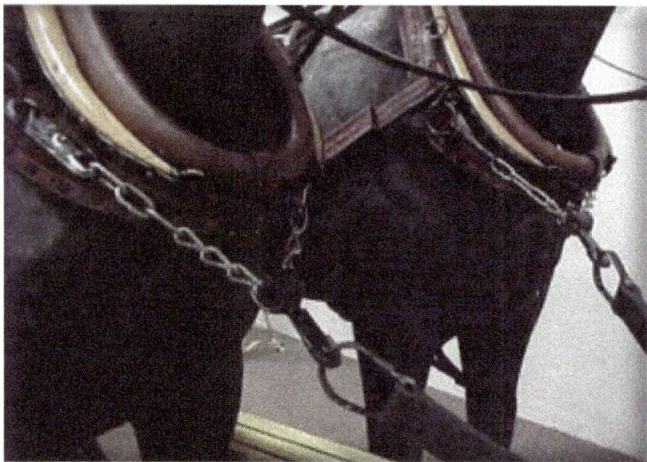

6 horse harness was packed in the coach. Russet harness was easier to clean. Wooden hames were less expensive. A sliding bracket on chain allowed for pole movement. Buckles were black.

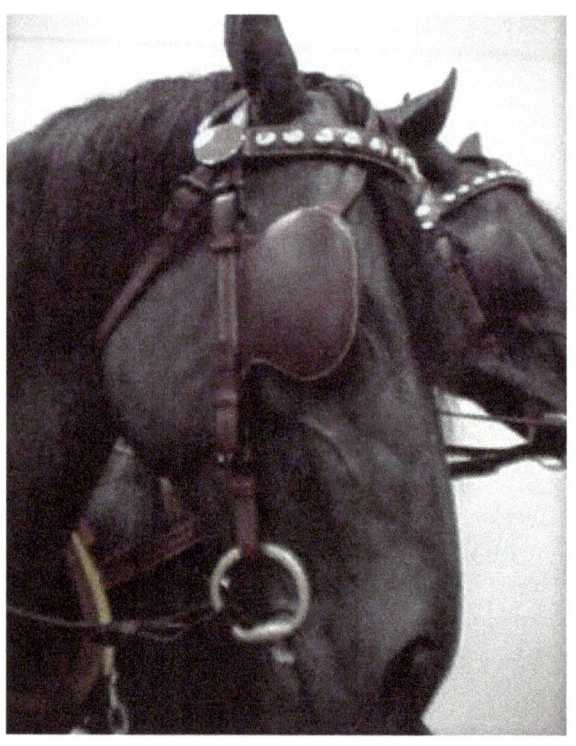

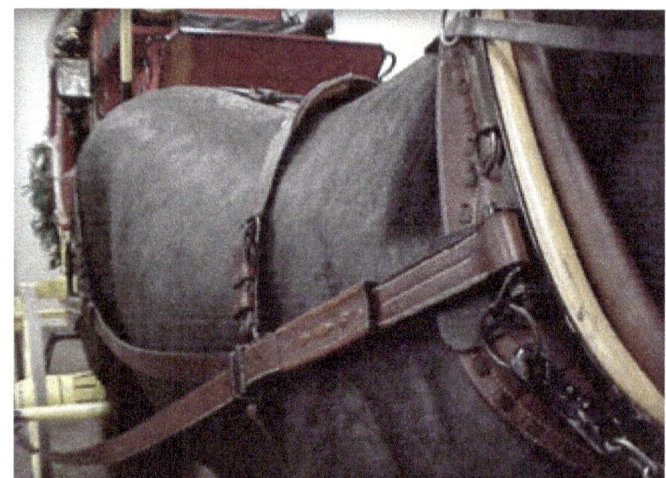

The wheelers harness had three buttons, the swing team two and the leaders one. The harness was made simple to easily fit most horses. The hitch was called a "loose hitch." This term refers to the fact that it did not restrict the movement of the horses over long distance travel.

COLORFUL CHARACTERS

MOUNTAIN MEN
"SOME PEOPLE FOLLOW WAGON TRACKS WHILE OTHERS BREAK NEW TRAILS."

Mountain men were trappers and explorers who roamed the North American Rocky Mountains. The populated areas grew from about 1810 through the 1880s with a peak population in the early 1840s. These mountain men were instrumental in opening up the various Emigrant Trails and widened trails into wagon roads allowing Americans in the east to settle the new territories of the far west. Organized wagon trains of settlers traveled over roads that had earlier been explored and charted by these mountain men. The mountain men and the big fur companies also originally opened these routes to serve the mule train based inland fur trade.

James Beckwourth, was a black man born into slavery. Beckwourth was freed by his master, who was also his father. He was a blacksmith apprentice before moving to the West to become a trapper. During his time on the frontier he lived with the Crow tribe, discovered the Beckwourth Pass in the Sierra Nevada Mountains during the CA Gold Rush, and expanded a trail which was used by thousands of settlers to reach California.

Kit Carson left Missouri as a young man to become a trapper and mountain man. He explored the West extensively, including the Rocky Mountains and Spanish California, along the way intermarrying with several tribes. His name became famous after being hired by John C. Fremont as an expedition guide and he was even featured as a hero in some western dime novels. Carson later served in the Mexican American War and Indian Wars, rising to the rank of Brigadier General despite being illiterate.

John "Grizzly" Adams earned his nickname more than anyone else has, by capturing and taming bears for zoos and circuses. One of his bears was even the model for the animal on the modern California state flag. Instead of relying on a rifle, Adams would frequently take on bears up close with nothing but his knife or even his hands alone. Despite his fearsome reputation, he captured most animals alive. While not an environmentalist by modern terms, Adams clearly loved the outdoors and was most at home there.

Jim Bridger was one of the major figures in winning the West. Bridger intermingled with several native tribes and could converse in French, Spanish and several tribal languages. He was an explorer at an early age and one of the first white men to see Yellowstone and the Great Salt Lake. He later entered the fur trade and married several native women. Even in his twilight years he left a legacy as a trailblazer and adventurer, creating an alternative route from Wyoming to Montana, and serving as an army scout.

John "Liver-eating" Johnson was born with the last name Garrison. As an underage soldier he served aboard a ship in the Mexican-American war, before striking an officer, deserting his post, and traveling to Montana to dig for gold. He gained his nickname according to a legend, when his Native American wife was killed by the Crow, he embarked on a vendetta against the tribe, killing several and cutting out their livers to consume. This was said to be an insult, as the Crow believed they'd be barred from the afterlife without a liver. His story, absent these grisly details, would inspire the Robert Redford film "Jeremiah Johnson."

Accompanying the Lewis and Clark expedition, **John Colter** is often credited as being the first mountain man. Considered one of the best hunters in the expedition group, he was constantly relied upon to feed the party. His skills as a guide were also treasured, and he helped the group traverse mountain passes and navigate rivers. After breaking from Lewis and Clark, Colter made a name for himself navigating the wilds of Wyoming unguided and in the dead of the winter. On a later expedition in Montana, Colter was also forced to flee naked and unarmed from Blackfoot braves, managing to evade capture after running for miles and even killing one of his pursuers.(cited from: https://www.wideopenspaces.com/10-badass-mountain-men-time/)

THE PONY EXPRESS
"POLISHING YOUR PANTS ON SADDLE LEATHER DON'T MAKE YOU A RIDER."

In April 1860, the famed Pony Express began using horse and rider relay teams to shuttle mail along a 2,000-mile route between St. Joseph, Missouri, and Sacramento, California in 10 days or less! The company only operated 19 months until the telegraph put an end to its need. Some of the riders of 1860-61 are better known than others. But it took all the riders to make this rigorous schedule happen.

Meet a few of the notable riders.

Johnny Fry was born in Kentucky and moved with his family to Missouri when he was 16 years old. Because he was an accomplished horseman, Alexander Majors asked him to ride for the Pony Express. After the Pony Express, Johnny enlisted in the army. He was killed at Baxter Springs where a huge monument salutes those buried there. He is attributed to be the first rider of the Pony Express.

Buffalo Bill Cody, who later became famous for his Wild West Show, was a rider for the Pony Express and wrote of his experiences. Another rider for the Pony Express was Wild Bill Hickok, a friend and mentor of Buffalo Bill. Both are well known, but few people know that they started their "careers" as Pony Express riders!

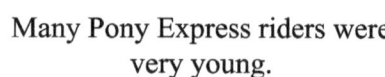

Many Pony Express riders were very young.

Billy Tate was a 14-year-old Pony Express rider who rode the express trail in Nevada near Ruby Valley. During the Paiute uprising of 1860 he was chased by a band of Paiute Indians on horseback and was forced to retreat into the hills behind some big rocks where he killed seven of his assailants in a shootout before being killed himself. His body was found riddled with arrows but was not scalped, a sign that the Paiutes honored their enemy.

Robert "Pony Bob" Haslam was one of the most daring riders for the Pony Express. He was first hired to help build stations and was then put on a run from Friday's Station to Buckland's Sation. His greatest ride, 120 miles in 8 hours and 20 minutes while wounded, was an important contribution to the fastest trip ever made by the Pony Express. Indian problems in 1860 led to Pony Bob Haslam's record-breaking ride. The mail carried Lincoln's inaugural address. After the telegraph line put the Express out of business, he worked for several stage lines. Pony Bob is buried in Chicago.

Jack Keetley was hired at the age of nineteen, and put on the run from Marysville to Big Sandy. He was a member of the Pony Express throughout its operations. Jack Keetley's longest ride, upon which he doubled back for another rider, ended at Seneca where he was taken from the saddle sound asleep. He had ridden 340 miles in 31 hours without stopping to rest or eat.

(cited from: https://nationalponyexpress.org/historic-pony-express-trail/1860-1861-history/ and http://www.eyewitnesstohistory.com/ponyexpress.htm and http://whoweareandwherewecamefrom.blogspot.com/2011/08/pony-express-in-my-family.html, https://deadlandsridersonthestorm.obsidianportal.com/wikis/the-pony-express)

Johnny Fry

Buffalo Bill Cody

Billy Tate

Pony Bob

Jack Keetley

STAGECOACH GUARDS AND DRIVERS
"CONFIDENCE IS THE FEELING YOU HAVE BEFORE YOU UNDERSTAND THE SITUATION."

Stagecoach robberies were frequent occurrences. Gold dust, gold bars, gold coins, legal papers, checks, and drafts were transported in the strongbox. The strongbox weighed from 100 to 150 pounds. Because they carried the most valuable assets of the West, these sturdy boxes – made of Ponderosa pine, oak and iron – were much sought after by bandits.

The real security of the strong boxes came from those who protected them—the Wells Fargo drivers and shotgun guards. The typical driver was a colorful character, about 40 years old, very competent with whip, often swaggering and rough-spoken, but always polite and courteous with ladies on board. They were "the kind of men you could depend on if you got into a fix," according to Wells Fargo detective Jim Hume. If would-be thieves were foolhardy enough to try to steal a treasure box in transit, they found themselves staring down the barrel of a sawed-off shotgun loaded with double-aught buckshot. (cited from: https://www.desertusa.com/ desert-people/wells-fargo.html)

Artist N.C. Wyeth painted "The Pay Stage"; a stage driver and the shotgun messenger, alert for danger on a moonlit western road.

The adventure and romance of western subjects captivated many artists, early filmmakers, and the American public in the early twentieth century. Nostalgia for the old West led to the popularity of Wells Fargo stagecoaches in community events.

Between 1870 and 1884, Wells Fargo stages were the target of 347 robbery attempts, an average of about 2 a month across the system. Getting the stage and its cargo through was not a job for the fainthearted, and some of the most respected lawmen in the West accepted the challenge. Among those who spent time driving and guarding stagecoaches were **Wyatt Earp, Morgan Earp, Wild Bill Hickok and William Fredrick "Buffalo Bill" Cody**. The term "riding shotgun" is still sometimes used today. (cited from: https://www.desertusa.com/desert-people/wells-fargo.html)

George Hackett was guarding Wells Fargo's treasure box containing $23,000 in gold on the LaPorte-Marysville stage in California on July 13, 1882, when a man with a shotgun and flour sack for a mask ordered the stage to halt. Hackett responded with a shotgun volley that knocked the robber's hat off and grazed his head before he fled. This was just one of the infamous Black Bart's robberies – and his closest call until his capture the following year. Hackett finished his route into Marysville. On the return trip later that day, the stage was held up again. Hackett thwarted the second robbery, too. (cited from: http://stories.wf.com/ wp-content/uploads/WF-historical-movember-mustaches.pdf)

Black Bart (whose real name was Charles E. Bolles) robbed 28 stagecoaches of their strongboxes in Northern California and Southern Oregon, but never touched a passenger. His trademark clothing was a linen duster and a flour-sack mask. He carried an unloaded shotgun and was also known for leaving the occasional poetry verse behind. Wells Fargo pressed charges only on his final robbery. At that robbery he left behind a handkerchief that had a laundry mark that was used to find him. Bolles was convicted and sentenced to 6 years in San Quentin Prison, but his stay was shortened to 4 years for good behavior. When released, reporters asked if he was going to rob anymore stagecoaches, Bolles replied "No gentlemen, I'm through with crime." And when asked if he would write more poetry. He laughed, "Now didn't you hear me say that I am through with crime?" Black Bart disappeared without a trace shortly after his release from prison. His San Francisco boarding house room was found vacated in February 1888, and the outlaw was never seen again. (cited from: https://www.thewildwest.org/cowboys/wildwestoutlawsandlawmen/173-blackbart)

Charley Parkhurst was a legendary driver of six-horse stagecoaches during California's Gold Rush — the "best whip in California," by one account. Parkhurst had the makeup for it: "short and stocky," a whiskey drinker, cigar smoker and tobacco chewer who wore a black eye patch after being kicked in the left eye by a horse. Charlie had one other attribute, this one carefully hidden from the outside world. When Parkhurst died in 1879 at age 67, near Watsonville, California, a doctor discovered that the famous stagecoach driver was a woman! Charley was Charlotte. She was considered one of the safest stagecoach drivers — not a daredevil, like so many of her contemporaries — and had a special rapport with the horses. She drove for Wells Fargo, at least once moving a large cargo of gold across the country. Parkhurst could claim one other distinction: an 1867 registry in Santa Cruz County lists a Charles Darkey Parkhurst from New Hampshire as having registered to vote — more than 50 years before the 19th Amendment gave women the right to vote.

One of the most famous stagecoach drivers was **Henry James Monk,** who drove the stage from Genoa, Utah to Placerville, California. Different names have been attributed to him, such as "Knight of the Lash," or the "King of Coachmen." Most people knew him as "Hank." He would drive stages at breakneck speeds along the winding Sierra mountain roads. Hank became famous for the ride he gave Horace Greeley, a journalist for the New York Daily Tribune, over the Sierra Nevada mountains, from Virginia City, to Placerville. Greeley had complained to his driver, Hank, that the trip was going too slowly and he needed to reach Placerville, where he had a lecture engagement. It seems the constant grumblings from Greeley caused the driver to speed up and drive his team furiously. When Greeley expressed his concerns about the breakneck pace, Hank replied, "Horace, keep your seat! I told you I would get there by five o'clock, and by God I'll do it, if the axles hold!" Though shaken from the tumultuous journey, Greeley did indeed arrive on time. As a token of gratitude, he awarded Hank with the finest suit Placerville had to offer. The ride took on a legendary status after Mark Twain caught wind of the tale and included his embellished retelling of it in his 1872 book, "Roughing It". (cited from: http://www.parks.ca.gov/pages/22491/files/ Those_Daring_Stage_Drivers.pdf)

Stage driver **"Shotgun" Taylor** never let winter blizzards keep him off the road. Dressed in a buffalo robe, coat and pants, Taylor drove the Wells Fargo stage between Salt Lake City and Montana gold mining camps. He once covered 450 miles in a record time of 66 hours—in summer. His nickname came from an incident when he pulled a short-barrel shot gun on a bully. (cited from: Wells Fargo' By Robert Joseph Chandler p.52)

Popular western stagecoach drivers had a style all their own. One of the most colorful was the celebrated fashionista **Jim Miller**. Even in an occupation notable for embroidered overcoats and flashy accessories, Miller's ostentatious style stood out. His hats were the widest Mormon wide-brims available, his ascot tie held in place by stick pins as large as a lady's brooch and his whip stock bound with bands of pure gold. Before Wells Fargo began adding armed guards, the stage driver was the only defense against attempted robbery. On one run in the mid-1860s, Miller set out with five passengers and $30,000 in minted gold for a mining payroll. As the stage slowed on a steep grade, the feared "Halt!" and a command to "Throw down the box!" growled from the tawny twilight. Miller recognized the danger and reacted without hesitation. He aimed a swinging blow with his buckskin lash at the near-wheel horse and in the same movement brandished a heavy dragoon revolver. Miller pulled the trigger and the dragoon roared like a cannon.

The Concord Coach rocked back and forth on its springs as the horses bolted, which may have helped everyone survive withering gunfire from bandits hidden in a ditch alongside the road. Bullets splintered the expensive enamel painting on the coach door as the passengers cowered on the floor, guzzling the last of the evening's rum. Miller's quick action saved the day and the stage thundered off into the darkness with the Wells Fargo treasure and passengers intact.

When word of Miller's bravery reached Wells Fargo's headquarters in San Francisco, the company announced that it would award him "the biggest bullion pocket watch and chain ever made." (cited from: https://thetahoeweekly.com/2018/05/dandy-jim-miller-stage-driver-with-style/)

WILD WEST SHOWS
"ALWAYS BE ABLE TO LOOK BACK AND SAY, 'AT LEAST I DIDN'T LEAD NO HUMDRUM LIFE'."

Born near LeClaire in Scott County, Iowa, in 1846, Buffalo Bill Cody rode on the Pony Express at the age of 14. During the American Civil War Cody first served as a Union scout in campaigns against the Kiowa and Comanche. In 1863 he enlisted with the Seventh Kansas Cavalry and saw action in Missouri and Tennessee. In 1867, he began buffalo hunting to feed construction crews building railroads; this is how he got the nickname that would define him forever.

In 1868, Cody returned to his work for the Army as chief of scouts. Cody acquired a reputation for accurate marksmanship. He also had total recall of the vast terrain he had traversed as well as knowledge of Indian ways. He was in demand as a scout and guide, mostly for the U.S. Fifth Cavalry. Cody, who frequently took dangerous assignments that others refused, was awarded the Medal of Honor for his heroic actions.

He became a national folk hero thanks to Ned Buntline's dime-novel exploits of his alter ego, "Buffalo Bill." In late 1872, Cody went to Chicago to make his stage debut in "The Scouts of the Prairie," which was one of Buntline's original Wild West shows. The next year, "Wild Bill" Hickok joined the show and the troupe toured for 10 years.

In 1883, Cody founded his own show, "Buffalo Bill's Wild West," a circus-like extravaganza that toured widely for 3 decades in the United States and later in Europe. He loved children and worked out plans for them to see his show for free! Besides Buffalo Bill himself, the Wild West show starred sharpshooter Annie Oakley and Chief Sitting Bull. Native Americans traveled around the United States and Europe as part of the show. They were able to wear tribal clothes and perform dances forbidden on the reservation – the Indians were able to represent themselves AND they were paid well! The show played at Queen Victoria's Golden Jubilee in 1887 and was staged throughout Europe. In 1893, 3,000,000 people attended the show during its tenure on the Midway adjacent to the official grounds of the World's Columbian Exposition in Chicago.

Buffalo Bill continued to perform in his Wild West show until 1916. He passed away in 1917. (cited from: https://www.biography.com/performer/buffalo-bill-cody https://www.britannica.com/biography/William-F-Cody)

THE REALITY
"AN OLD TIMER IS A MAN WHO'S HAD A LOT OF INTERESTING EXPERIENCES-SOME OF THEM TRUE."

Wild West Shows, dime novels and later, movies and TV, often depicted the settling of the West as a wonderful adventure. Many tales were spun around the campfire to exaggerate and glamorize the reality. There was some reality in the story-telling though. Buffalo Bill used Concord Coaches in his Wild West Shows and old western movies, filmed in the 1930s and 1940s, usually used authentic, old Concord Coaches in their scenes. You can watch some of the older westerns to see crashes in which the movie studios filmed these antique coaches running off cliffs and smashing into the canyons below. You won't see that in modern westerns as the original coaches are now worth hundreds of thousands of dollars each, but the stories in the old western movies and dime-novels were adventurous - and many times true!

Riding on a stagecoach was anything but glamorous as many movies depict. Passengers were told, "Don't imagine for a moment that you're going on a picnic. Expect annoyance, discomfort and hardships. If you are disappointed, thank heaven."

Only a bit of luggage was allowed. Mail had first priority inside the coach if the weather was bad. Motion sickness was expected.

Be first to board the coach!

Eighteen to thirty days of "pinched up, jammed in and screwed down misery"

A grand adventure intermixed with fear

AND STILL TODAY, THROUGH A MIST OF TIME THEY COME

Gloria Austin driving the Austin Coach.

GLOSSARY

If yer' gonna ride, know the language. Here's a few Stagecoach Terms and Slang of the Old West.

Boot – A deep luggage carrier at the rear of a stagecoach and also under the driver's seat.
Box – The stage driver's seat.
Brother Whip – The stagecoach driver, also called simply "Whip."
Bull-Whacker – A driver of a freight wagon, usually with oxen.
Carry-all – A light, covered carriage that could hold several people.
Celerity Wagon – A stagecoach used in rough country, also referred to as a mud wagon.
Charlie – A stagecoach driver.
Concord Coach – A stagecoach made by Abbott, Downing Company, in Concord, New Hampshire.
Conductor – The person who rode with the driver of a stagecoach and collected fares, took care of passengers and was responsible for the mail.
Corduroy Road – A road created by logs laid across a swampy, low-lying area, placed together or "ribbed" like corduroy cloth.
Division – 250 miles of trail belonging to a superintendent on the Overland Route.
Division Agent – The person in charge of 250 miles of road on the Overland Route, also called Superintendent. They were in charge of purchasing animals and equipment, maintaining the stations, and hiring station keepers, conductors, hostlers, drivers, and blacksmiths.
Drag – An object attached to the back of a stagecoach to slow it when going downhill.
Expressman – A messenger carrying express items.
Groom – A stableman, one who takes care of the horses
Hame – One of two curved bars fitted to a horse collar, holding the traces of a harness.
Hangers-on – A phrase used by the more "well-off" riding inside the stagecoach, referring to those who were riding on top.
Home Station – A larger station where meals and lodging were provided to passengers.
Hostlers – Took care of the horses and mules at the stage stops, as well as changing the team.
Jehu – A stagecoach driver, taken from the name of a Biblical character who drove fast and furiously.
Johnnycake – A type of cornbread often provided to travelers at stage stops.
Leaders – The two front animals of the team. These would be the smallest, smartest and most alert of the team.
Lines – Reins.
Near – Referred to the horses or mules on the left side of the team, furthest from the driver.
Off – Referred to the horses or mules on the right side of the team, nearest the driver.
Overland – Across land rather than by water.

Postrider – A person who carried the post, or mail, on horseback.
Relay – A team of horses or mules kept in readiness at a way station to relieve the team of an approaching stagecoach.
Reaches – Bars that connected the rear axles with the forward part of the coach.
Reinsman – A stagecoach driver.
Ribbons – Reins.
Rig – Harness.
Road Agent – A stagecoach robber.
Run – The distance between stage stations.
Shotgun – A stagecoach guard. Also referred to as a "Shotgun Messenger."
Singletree – A horizontal crossbar, to the ends of which the traces of a harness are attached.
Stagehorn – A horn or bugle blown by the conductor as the stage neared the station
Stageline – A stagecoach company.
Stagers – The men who ran or owned the stage business.
Staging – The business of carrying people and mail by stagecoach.
Station – The place at which a stagecoach stopped.
Station Keeper – The person in charge of the station stop.
Superintendent – The person in charge of 250 miles of road on the Overland Route, also called Division Agent.
Swing Station – A small stage station where the team was changed. Usually consisting of little more than a small cabin and barn or corral, it usually manned by just a few stock-tenders. Stages stopped at Swing Stations for about ten minutes before moving on.
Swingers – If a team had six animals, the two in the middle were called swingers and were easily controlled by the other two pairs as they did their work leading or stabilizing.
Team – The horses or mules pulling the stagecoach, usually consisting of four to six animals.
Thorough Brace – A leather strap of many layers that supported the body of the stagecoach.
Traces – The side straps by which a horse pulls the stagecoach.
Transcontinental – Across the United States
Turnpike – The main road on which travelers paid a toll or fee
Way Station – Same as a station.
Waybills – Stage line advertisements posted in towns and villages.
Wheelers – The two animals at the rear of the team. These would be the largest and strongest animals to provide stability nearest the coach.
Wheelwright – A person who makes of fixes wheels.
Whip – The stagecoach driver, also called "Brother Whip."
Whippletree – The horizontal bar at the front of the stagecoach, to which single trees are attached.

SOURCES

THE LURE OF THE WEST
https://www.franciscanmedia.org/saint-junipero-serra/
https://carmelmission.org/visit/st-junipero-serra/

GETTING TO THE WEST
https://en.wikipedia.org/wiki/Central_Overland_Route
https://en.wikipedia.org/wiki/Old_Spanish_Trail_(trade_route)
https://en.wikipedia.org/wiki/Butterfield_Overland_Mail
https://www.legendsofamerica.com/mo-stlouis/
https://www.stlouis-mo.gov/government/departments/planning/cultural-resources/preservation-plan/Part-I-St-Louis-and-the-American-West.cfm

GETTING SUPPLIES AND PEOPLE TO THE WEST
https://nationalcowboymuseum.org/explore/hoofs-wheels-transportation-west/
http://www.stagecoachfreightwagon.org/NSFWA/vehicle_freight-wagon.html
https://www.hansenwheel.com/resources/faqs-wagon-history#hitch
http://www.wheelsthatwonthewest.com/Pages/Featured_Vehicle_Pride_St_Louis.html
http://oldphotoarchive.com/stories/inside-a-pioneer-covered-wagon
http://idaho.untraveledroad.com/Blaine/Ketchum/50WSign.htm
http://www.wheelsthatwonthewest.com/Pages/ArticlesMilitaryEscortWagons.html
https://www.legendsofamerica.com/ca-20muleteams/
https://www.hansenwheel.com/history-of-the-army-wagon
https://en.wikipedia.org/wiki/Cumberland_Pontoons
http://www.wadehamptoncamp.org/pontoon.html
https://www.loc.gov/item/2018666586/
https://helenair.com/lifestyles/crosscut/the-diary-of-a-civil-war-era-ambulance/article_ff97df94-3151-550c-9d3f-7bb587b10050.html
http://www.civilwarmed.org/evacuation/
https://www.fortpierre.com/attractions/norman-signs-fort-pierre-deadwood-trail/
https://www.blackhillsknowledgenetwork.org/home/the-many-trails-into-deadwood-helped-make-history.html

https://www.mtexpress.com/wood_river_journal/special_sections/the-story-behind-ketchum-s-famous-ore-wagons/article_b2709ea4-89e5-11e7-bbdf-4febd933bfc1.html

https://www.berksmontnews.com/opinion/the-historian-six-horse-bell-teams/article_d18af4c7-05d4-5c32-a7af-89ed696e452f.html
https://www.encyclopedia.com/history/united-states-and-canada/us-history/wagon-train

ABBOTT and DOWNING
https://www.burgumfamily.co.uk/pdf_books/John_Burgum_Merri_Ferrell.pdf

GETTING AROUND IN THE WEST
https://www.parks.ca.gov/?page_id=25449
http://www.nhd.uscourts.gov/sites/default/files/ci/exhibits/tour/floor-one-exhibits/the-concord-coach.aspx
https://www.legendsofamerica.com/wells-fargo/
http://www.wyomingtalesandtrails.com/stagelines2.html
https://truewestmagazine.com/celerity-mud-wagons/
https://www.legendsofamerica.com/we-deadwoodstage/

COLORFUL CHARACTERS
https://www.wideopenspaces.com/10-badass-mountain-men-time/
https://nationalponyexpress.org/
http://www.eyewitnesstohistory.com/ponyexpress.htm
http://whoweareandwherewecamefrom.blogspot.com/2011/08/pony-express-in-my-family.html
https://www.legendsofamerica.com/we-oldwestwisdom/
https://www.desertusa.com/desert-people/wells-fargo.html
http://stories.wf.com/wp-content/uploads/WF-historical-movember-mustaches.pdf
https://www.thewildwest.org/cowboys/wildwestoutlawsandlawmen/173-blackbart
Wells Fargo By Robert Joseph Chandler
https://www.nytimes.com/2018/12/05/obituaries/charley-parkhurst-overlooked.html
http://www.parks.ca.gov/pages/22491/files/Those_Daring_Stage_Drivers.pdf
https://thetahoeweekly.com/2018/05/dandy-jim-miller-stage-driver-with-style/
https://www.biography.com/performer/buffalo-bill-cody
https://www.britannica.com/biography/William-F-Cody
http://www.codyenterprise.com/news/people/article_4b3c-2cba-86a4-11e7-b29c-7bec6692e53e.html
https://deadlandsridersonthestorm.obsidianportal.com/wikis/the-pony-express